London
Street Map

Whitehall Jackals

Whitehall Jackals

Chris McCabe & Jeremy Reed

ISBN: 978-0-9573847-2-9

Scan QR code for further title information

First published April 2013 by:

Nine Arches Press
Great Central Studios
92 Lower Hillmorton Rd
Rugby, Warwickshire
CV21 3TF

www.ninearchespress.com

Printed in Britain by:

imprintdigital.net
Seychelles Farm,
Upton Pyne,
Exeter
EX5 5HY
www.imprintdigital.net

Whitehall Jackals

Chris McCabe & Jeremy Reed

A London Collaboration

Nine
Arches
Press

Chris McCabe was born in Liverpool in 1977. His previous collections are *The Hutton Inquiry, Zeppelins* and *THE RESTRUCTURE* (all with Salt Publishing). His work has been described by *The Guardian* as "an impressively inventive survey of the uses of English in the early 21st century". He has recorded a CD with the Poetry Archive and has had work included in numerous anthologies including *Identity Parade: New British and Irish Poets* (Bloodaxe, 2010), *The Captain's Tower: seventy poets celebrate Bob Dylan at seventy* (Seren, 2011), *Adventures in Form* (Penned in the Margins, 2012) and *Dear World & Everyone in it* (Bloodaxe, 2013). His plays *Shad Thames, Broken Wharf* (also published by Penned in the Margins as a limited edition box) and *Mudflats* have been performed in London and Liverpool. He works as the Poetry Librarian at The Saison Poetry Library and teaches for The Poetry School.

Jeremy Reed has been for decades one of Britain's most dynamic, adventurous and controversial poets; *The Independent* called him "British poetry's glam, spangly, shape-shifting answer to David Bowie". He has published over 40 books of poetry, fiction and non-fiction, winning prestigious literary prizes such as the Somerset Maugham Award, and, on coming to live in London in the 1980s, was patronised by the artist Francis Bacon. Amongst his fans are J.G. Ballard, Pete Doherty and Bjork who has called his work "the most beautiful, outrageously brilliant poetry in the world". His poetry publications in recent years include *Heartbreak Hotel* (Orion), *Duck and Sally Inside, This Is How You Disappear* (both Enitharmon), *West End Survival Kit* (Waterloo Press), *Bona Drag* (Shearsman) and *Piccadilly Bongo* with Marc Almond (Enitharmon), and his most recent novels are *The Grid* (Peter Owen) and *Here Comes the Nice* (Chomu Press). Jeremy Reed also works and performs with musician Itchy Ear as The Ginger Light.

CONTENTS

Where the City round me celebrates the triumph of the brain
Of man over his darkness, in the effervescent blaze
Of a commerce-sponsored carnival of multicoloured bulbs.

David Gascoyne
from *Night Thoughts*

CODA PREFIX: ACCELERATED URBAN HIGHS

Chris McCabe and I first met physically in the subsurface, low-lit, book-stacked basement at Red Snapper Books, 22 Cecil Court WC2N, a cutting-edge counterculture bookshop I fronted with inimitable style for its owner, Aaron Budnik, and where he'd come to look at rare stock as possible purchases for the Poetry Library, if the cost could be compressed into his squeezed budget. Already enthusiastic readers of each other's work, we immediately established a sympathetic chemistry, talking of the essentially non-mainstream poets we admired: the Black Mountain hipsters Ed Dorn and Robert Duncan, post-modern gossipy New Yorkers like Frank O'Hara and John Ashbery, the British tearaway language-drenched Barry MacSweeney, the speed in Tom Raworth's off-message snapshots, Iain Sinclair's capital psychogeographics, J.H. Prynne's forensically-cold financial investor's diction; stuff that rocked because it had elbowed attitude and didn't fit with the more generically-based social commentary that infects so much pedestrian British poetry. To me, if a poem doesn't radically alter your sensory experience of the world and recreate it, then it's of no interest, and if it doesn't risk shooting holes in the corruptly-maintained system, it lacks dialect with subverting politics through its alternative imaginative equivalent.

Shortly after our first meeting, quite literally below the street, I reviewed Chris' second collection *Zeppelins* (Salt, 2008) with zingy chutzpah, for David Caddy's magazine *Tears in the Fence*, noting particularly the rich and often crunched linguistic energies at work, and the concentrated focus on London as place of sourcing the poems. I wrote the review at First Out café/bar, St Giles High Street, back of the monolithic Centre Point and facing Renzo Piano's Central Saint Giles opposite, as one of the many West End locales where I regularly multitask; writing poetry, fiction and non-fiction at different periods of the day, as impulse directs the work's energised resourceful thrust, shifting me correspondingly to different writing places all over Soho, brokering not only poetry, but a highly individual look.

The idea of collaborating with Chris on a book of poetry resulting directly from London as our creative experiential basis came up in December 2010 — our Russian freeze, no-colour skies winter, and was quickly activated in January 2011, all contact and exchange of poems done electronically, as we fed off each other's accelerated dynamic to get the fired-up collab completed in three months. Knowing my intense concentration on speed — the reason to write one book is to start another, my neuronal energies are always hyper — we comfortably fitted the project into the duration we'd agreed. The title *Whitehall Jackals* came out of our mutual disgust with Tony Blair's war atrocities in Iraq, together with his oligarchical political regime of czars, spin, deception and pathological lies, all conveniently left unopposed by non-reactive mainstream British poetry.

What I've done, almost singularly, for a long time is to place poetry in an interactive role with the capital. By continuously writing my books in public spaces — cafes, outside in the street, sitting at the foot of the Seven Dials needle, on the plinth of the stone pagoda in China Town's Newport Place, on Blake's steps in Marshall Street, on buses — the act invariably, as it's done by hand, invites fixated attention, conversation, and the friendships created by accidental meetings with strangers has formed an integral part of my London life. When I first came to live in London in the early eighties, I'd write quite literally on the black railings at Piccadilly Circus, and I met half the world there, in terms of people I find interesting, some of whom became patrons.

Never compromise, and look like what you do has always been my pioneering dictum, so there's no separation between the individual and the work. Both Chris and I have little or no respect for academic poets — formal desk practitioners — I'd much rather have Pete Doherty's subversively-streetwise but inherently romantic lyrics; and the collaboration on *Whitehall Jackals*, done exclusively by email, involved minimal comment, zero criticism, no meetings, just consolidated support and encouragement carried by the work's momentum, and complete individual freedom of subject matter on both our parts to scope London according to our personal obsessions and associative identification with place.

London, so physicalised in history, so continually morphed into reinvention that it has no stable frontiers other than what's directly in your face — the rest is submerged face-lifted past — is for me most valuable for the randomised meetings it provides anywhere, anytime. The strangers I met in the course of working on this book are just one of the rewards of writing in public, as performance, and as a sort of implicit importuning that fascinates and attracts. As it chanced, Chris' obsessions lie more east of my west, so a balance was unintentionally established as to where we most incisively accessed individual territories.

What made this project additionally exciting was our complete creative freedom, working without an advance, publisher, or preconceived mapping of the territory, to be liberated into spontaneous uptake by each other's respective obsessions, mine often more personal than Chris', and to following a learning curve, in my case the increased realisation of the value of found material as it comes up with such full-on power.

Writing poetry is in part about using what you see that others usually let go or simply don't attach significance to. Living in London's a bit like watching and participating simultaneously in a real-time movie, and continually editing live footage to avoid saturation. If the capital's unstoppable energies feed directly into neural response, when you're writing outside, with the sniff of the real on constant overload, then the work is always on the point of shattering. If you're a London poet you've preferably got to be streetwise, have your own sympathetic milieu and give attitude to what you get. I've written poems on the backs of a pile of laundered bank notes that a friend produced from a re-sewn jacket interior for kicks — violet Pentel scoring blush-pink fifties — and to me it's all part of working London life to its edges. What you write on becomes the surface of your nerves, and for me it's always paper, organic converted to digital later, the physical as primary energy because it's work motivated by the eye and hand.

Our collaborative book, with its predominantly psychogeographic focus, a defiantly-intransigent leftfield indie whack at the city's towers, alleys, oxidised bridges, outlaw heroes, wharves, piss-churning river, commercialised shopping zones, and the whole psychotic London bubble compressed into the area within the orbital M25 motorway, all 610 square miles of hallucinated urban multiverse, is a series of transient signs, almost like personalised graffiti tags, pointing to the specific moment in time we engaged in this project. It catches London now, as it clicks on the supercharged senses of two committed poets, simultaneously each writing other books and doing the different things you do in a city.

What I learnt most from Frank O'Hara, as relevant to this book, is that you can make almost anything into subject matter for poetry, no matter how apparently ordinary, taboo, weird, shopaholic branded, accidentally found, state of the moment, colour blocked, it'll do. Chris McCabe and I have tried in *Whitehall Jackals* to break laws rather than observe them — isn't that the best reason to write? — to disrupt convention and become in the process edgewalkers.

Whitehall Jackals comprises the first of a proposed two-book London collaboration — once isn't sufficient — twice is right for this shape-shifting, language-crunching, edgy, subversive partnership. We'll be seeing you, I hope, reading and performing from the book, and you could also be seeing me around, why not try 3pm Soho's Newport Place, and I'll give you the handwritten poem I'm writing if you're interested, it's all part of what I do in a day, make poetry out of everything I see and feel: or try Seven Dials, under the needle at noon, Starbucks St Martin's Lane 2pm, First Out café mid-afternoon, or find me by the river on a foggy day. I'm the one in a stylishly-angled beret and the MAC Studio Fix foundation. See you when.

JR

WATERLOO

In search of a therapist
I took your route, the room
you led me to sedated
with Kandinsky. In the arches
mice looped arthritic fires,
hungover in deep reds
I walked
beneath silver rafters
counting in the steel grilles
your OXO of pigeons
weaving through the day-
returners with no records
of off-peak suburbia
until I entered the approach
to the Thames & found this love-
letter face-down in fragments :

I THINK THAT I'M OVER YOU
I'VE BEEN SAYING I AM FOR YEARS
BUT THE TRUTH IS DESPITE THE FACT
WE'VE NOT BEEN FRIENDS FOR OVER
TWO YEARS NOW NOT A DAY HAS
PASSED IN THE PAST 2000 DAYS
SINCE WE FIRST MET THAT I HAVEN'T
THOUGHT ABOUT YOU I FORGAVE
YOU BEFORE YOU EVEN APOLOGISED
I NEVER HATED YOU

.

commuters lay down your records like this

CM

FLEET

A black network in London's thalamus,
a landscaped-over solid trawl
licking a trace into Dead Dog Basin,
like a path-lab procedure,
a subterranean autopsy

of body parts in soup, bottles and dogs,
a swirly ooze down to Kentish Town loch
and under to St Pancras,
furred arteries pushing to King's Cross
as cold bacterial soup, a mucky rush

that puddles on the road sometimes
in thunder-rain at Holborn and Blackfriars
in think-bubbles, the river's secret life
come up to be decoded like intelligence
and splashed through by the tube exit,

I'll never know I've walked it home
in squidgy traces on the floor
at South Hill Park like a liquid barcode.
We talk about the river's drop
at the Magdala, drunk out of the rain

in leaf-slidy November, the street
wallpapered over by stripped orange leaves;
and someone claims they've fucked beside its source,
the bottomless pool by the aqueduct
power-pointing into the river

to feel its drive into the underground,
but it's not clear where water starts,
unlike a road, its shoplifting impulse
traffics into a dark gritty corridor.
We stand above it as we talk,

a disturbed system of tunnels and tubes,
aquifers, islanded from the rain,
and I can feel the drop under my feet
into the Fleet pit, as I buy a round
and feel the fourth or fifth light up my brain.

JR

VAUXHALL BRIDGE

L'uomo Vogue met me in White City
At the photographer's terrace
Past the analogue estate of the BBC
Last night's prosecco flat in the kitchen
The photographer made tea
His assistant asked questions
The women of *L'uomo* arrived late
— turbot-white in the cheeks —
Fed on cherries & cocaine
They made a dressing room of the lounge
And started to dress me
One said "They speak of you so highly in London"
The other "Italian is such a beautiful language"
We took a cab over Vauxhall Bridge
The photographer hung-up on his daughter
I'd timed the tide & they walked me in
The photographer shouted "grab the stick"
The police tug stopped mid-tide
The assistant developed negatives in rock-pools
They walked me to the stone lion to stroke its verdigris mane
With clothes I didn't own
MI6 watched as the photographer said "lay down on the lion
like — I don't know — you've fallen asleep"
— green light from Millbank across the river —
They gave me towels — Shelley undrowned at Alembic House —
In the pub the women asked "what do you drink" I said Guinness
And they took a cab to the next shoot
— a warehouse in Shoreditch. For weeks
I walked the bookshops of Oxford Street

In search of news from Italy
I thought of Pound in a tent, *The Cantos*,
When the issue arrived the Thames was absent,
No poet in its pages :
A musician in a warehouse, an auteur in some trees.

CM

West Enders

We're mostly in dispersal and regroup
in alleys, bars, a recessed court —
I met you today on Great Chapel Street
(OS grid TQ295815)
back from your urinalysis
Trimethoprin pills in a labelled pot

and it was synchronicity
ripped an orange shooting-star through my brain:
our chance encounter leading to a bar,
the spiral Dog and Duck on Bateman Street —
your habit reconfirmed, the drug
coming up like a red quasar

signalling in your chemistry.
East's low-key residential, tangy docks,
our West End's speed — impacting momentum,
everything shattered at speed of light,
the body bulleting through G-forces
on a trajectory that turns out right.

Soho attracts like a gravity-well,
a short story that's always incomplete
and seems to centre on Ham Yard
or Marshall Street for plot. We give it juice
looking for a secret room underground
where it all happens and the singer's voice

confirms the change. I'm busy in my grid,
nitrogen dioxide 40 ppb
as a heavy-metal blood carrier,
pulling a face or poem from the crowd
as I do on Shaftesbury Avenue
submerged by white noise — there's no second time

the street's the same, but I look out for you
as someone new in my anthology
of chosen ones, a red light facing down
the edgy traffic, as I point into
a 5pm turned pink in hazy arcs,
my body egg-whisked by adrenalin.

JR

WAPPING OLD STAIRS

A lighter, a camera, a PLUMS bottle
— MACKINTOSH BROS. —
washes in the tide at the Old Stairs :
I smash the bottle against ceramic & brick
— no message but ink —
the content oozes conger black
slicks wet in ebony nox
gluts in chunks its obsidian soup,
the river's bed condensed to wet ash
— no message —
the camera ejects the card,
digital images crust in wet clay
embedded with the river's source.
I take the lighter & camera —
past Tower Bridge a courier sits
on the pavement — head between knees —
opened envelopes around his feet,
two Latino men shine the bullion
of the Tate & Lyle logo
— *out of the strong came forth sweetness* —
as cigar smoke rises like cremations
of vermin. At Dark Horse Walk
a payroll manager stares out the tide's volta,
pockets an Identity Card, folds up collars —
I scratch the wheel of the lighter :
its wet flint adds nothing to this

CM

24

WHITEHALL ENDGAME

(depleted uranium mix)

The 5pm sky's like rainy sapphires
a blue toxic hydrocarbon blanket,
and you're my pick-up, bite my lip
to redden like a strawberry.
It's later in accelerated endgame time
by 600 seconds than when we met
at the compressed Starbucks on Hollen Street,
you a Beijing space-time interloper
put into a blonde-bobbed Eurasian mix.

The psychopathic jackal Tony Blair,
four blacked-out Range Rovers gunned
through town, a war criminal's carbon tail
choking polluted haze, his handgun grin
cold as forensics, czar to every war's
genocide, the killer autocrat
smeared in depleted uranium, Gulf blood,
the meltdown hedge funder — the commandant
guarded 24/7 by thugs in suits,
Glock pistols in their Paul Smith repertoire.

We watch his cars open a corridor
into a cannibalistic future —
Blair crunches Cherie for a final meal.
The day builds on us like a pyramid
of neural info — *love me to the end
of Soho village* — there's no other way
sighting those tyres that leave blood on the bend.

JR

BLOOMSBURY

for Kelvin Corcoran

It's the music of what *matters*
it pulls me this way always
across Waterloo Bridge
in search of the poet
— revenant of sliproad hymns —
the Isle of Dogs smatters
its SIM cards to the stars
as Westminster descales
gold florins
in the Counting House
of the river's pummelling,
the Aldwych arcs a scythe against
Bush House & pushes me north
— in search of the poet —
through the contented Squares
of Tavistock, Russell, Bloomsbury,
where my mind lost its trace —
night air around Gt. Ormond St
when my son was strung with fluids
like a doll in a rockpool
I walk that way through reduced serotonin
to the glyphs of SWEDENBORG HALL
inside the poet sings
with a haemorrhage on his mind —
adds his message to the city's signs :
the dark enfolding road we leave behind

CM

YAUATCHA

A blue light-box, deep sea ultramarine,
an Yves Klein shot with toothpaste blue
(Colgate Oxygen) faces out
on Broadwick Street, a rainy Sunday fuzz
pixelating beadily, a damp glow
grainy Soho 4pm 30/11 chill
we take inside from reflective windows
of Cowling & Wilcox opposite.
(I make adjustments for altered place states
in my sci-fi Soho novel *The Grid*)
and find immersion in 150 teas
and choose a Pau Dragon Orchid, scent
written into the name, a gold sauna
poured in a cup, a steamy tangy trick
turned on the palate — it's your green tea cake —
three leaf-green suitcases pitted in mousse
like baggage angled on the carousel
arrests my eye, an arty rococo detail
designed to tease the bite: the Cantonese
next to us fork venison puffs
and lobster dumplings, slowly, incisively
like surgery, a serious graft
of separating textures, while I stare
out at a 6ft strip of afternoon
leaked in with shop lights, frontage, drizzled smear,
a Broadwick Street industrial grey different
from any other Soho grey
and feel the transient suspense, the last
shot-down blues bled out of the winter day.

JR

Elephant & Castle

It's a top-deck 176 situation at Elephant & Castle
the bottle rolls against my shoes
METHADONE 100ML. AILMENT 2 OF 14. MAY CAUSE
DROWSINESS. DO NOT OPERATE
MACHINERY OR DRINK ALCOHOL.
I can see everything from here except sobriety :
communities that have themselves bought-out in glass.

You only age like this in the all the time I don't see you :
so spend some time with us. Spend it like tokens
for kiosks that sell loose cigarettes. Spend it like drains.
Spend it like hard water down the Victorian water-mains.
Spend it like the Shard's doubling of stars. Spend it like
something light to read on the commuter's underpass :
A Beginner's Guide to Property & Culture.

Page 54 has a picture of an estate agent reading Chekhov
in a dressing room. If you don't see me tonight I got off
at the Nag's Head next to the Barclays.

And folded myself in the Night Safe for you.

CM

WENLOCK ARMS

A summer there in sticky warehouse heat,
our fuzzy light-polluted sweat-drenched thrust
to monetize a dead friend's books
boxed into dusty architectural blocks,
dealers categorising firsts and states
Red Snapper partners itchy for hot cash
both of us maintaining dandified looks
in repurposed high-end Shoreditch,
its rogue outtake the Wenlock Arms
looking like a Krays' gang operation,
peeling green walls, purple frontage —
I'd knock at 10am for Aaron's flaky need
to stabilize, a drinks top-up
kicking the pineal with a sugared boot.
12 handpumps, a stripped-down defiant room
yeasty with real ale, I stepped into
a throwback parallel space-time
scrutinized for my beret and paste rings
crowding in starburst clusters at the bar —
an edgy glitter, a moody lagoon.
She never spoke, just handed me the glass.
Two months, two hours a day deconstructing
solid book tons as physicals, we sold
into profit — I kept a CA shelf
of Robert Duncan, orange sunshine
stored in the pages, had a last drink there
like flipping back to 1958.

Got all my times wrong, bussed back into town.
Knowing I'd be too early, or too late.

JR

EXECUTION DOCK

I used to stretch the city to elastics
now it's stone-set
scouring brickwork for a Capital E
— de-voweled pirates at Execution Dock —
the present site of Savill's estate agents
asphyxiated with a shortened rope
beneath lead-crossed windows in beet-red
the hanging bar above CERTIFICATE
FOR TENANCY DEPOSIT SCHEME
— the drop insufficient to break the neck —
access blocked with white vans
to the steps at Swan Wharf : tectonics of surveillance :
MARINE POLICING UNIT UNDERWATER &
CONFINED SPACE SEARCH TEAM
hung limbs barn-jig the Marshal's dance
agitations of sinews like a rubber squid
only a name with online epitaphs suffused with hits
— say Captain Kidd — can consider
a 4 BED PENTHOUSE ST KATHERINE DOCK
his gibbeted corpse cindering for twenty years
by the river in an iron cage
intestines billowed outwards in the salt-wash
then tied slack to a calcium mast of bone
the rest of the convicts marched across
the Thames from Marshalsea Prison
— including a white man, a Spaniard & a mulatto —
        this is no joke
to peruse the following with a priest
— who hears no confession —

the future laid out in converted Three Beds
CINNIBAR WHARF 695 PER WEEK
TOWER BRIDGE WHARF 495 PER WEEK
HALCYON WHARF 500 PER WEEK
low-key corpses swing like marrow-packed jute
until three high-tides wash over their heads

CM

BUYING STONES BOOTLEGS AT THE STABLES

Reconstructed yard, a Camden squeeze,
snuck back of a smudgy sage-green canal,
it's punchy in the cold, breath atomised
into blue hexagonal puffs —
vaporised carbon dioxide diamonds
signposting dispersed energies. I pick

my way in segues through the compressed crush,
Spanish, French, platinum Slovakians
freezing the moment with camera-phones
into a digital shoplift. The rush
keeps peaking: back of the Thai noodle stalls
I find my dealer and I want the lot,

69-78 outtakes, live
raw garage at Olympic — hooty sounds
riffed by a blues Al Qaeda with a look
that's generic defiant attitude,
biro-barrel skinny, punk Londoners
skinning convention alive like a mule,

smashing their carbon footprint on the globe.
The market accelerates to a jam,
slow-motion foot traffic full on by 3,
there's Amy Winehouse in ripped skinny jeans
looking like she's been up a century
and arrived tomorrow or yesterday

in personal space-time. I talk up wants
as needs: a 68 Chelsea rehearsal,
a casual slouch through river-muddy blues
at Cheyne Walk with hazy mist
throwing striptease figures over the bridge.
We share green tea in a blue paper cup

branded Caffe Nero: the day breaks up
in busy schedule: I go off with sounds
lifted from other times for completion,
go sit back to a wall by the canal's
oozy steps — and a tug churns into view
frothing white water and called Baby Blue.

JR

KING'S STAIRS, ROTHERHITHE

On Redriff Stairs Pepys diarised the beauty of a Plain
Girle : *one of the prettiest faces that we think we ever saw in
our lives.* Three centuries later, in a warehouse across the
bricked-up marshes, Bowie sashed blue his face for
Bermondsey. If this isn't how culture works, someone
shove a codex into history. *The Anathemata* is one answer
as David Jones mined his family out of Redriff to ask : *Did
he tie up across the water or did she toss at the Surrey shore?
Had he business at Dockhead?* Yes : Lady Stardust. The traces
are wan in February's summer. Fred Flinstone is the
crayola face of protest : STOP THAMES WATER RUINING
OUR PARK. Once established that the Thames Path is
an artifice in broken flow — access stutters through
padlocked gates, an underpass of dead-ends — then the
only solution is prose. Brunel's tower is a phallic umbril for
cigarette stumps. *OUR* PARK breaks its definitions —
KING'S STAIRS GARDENS — NO DOGS NO FOULING
NO DRINKING NO FIRES NO VEHICLES. We followed
the WiKi-map so how can we have lost the Elephant?
Like the Pilgrim Fathers back for a brew on St. Mary's
Estate. The Stairs have been quango'd into council bricks
as a chain tests the yield of moss in the lung-rut of the
tide. What we walk above — cling to hollow-steel not to
slip — is always the signed-off end of *project*. The defeater
of *petition*. Across the tide to Wapping we first see the
warehouses, then the apartments inside the warehouses,
then beyond them the skyline concertinas of estates. The
top floors open on gull-perspectives that no-one wants
to pay for. At our feet the moss only grows so far. First
there was a Jubilee & then I was born : the Thameside

glyphs make facts of my shoes. A Benetton bouquet locks its floral knots on the rails & in tribute the chalk scores : DARREN RIP   OUR PAL XX   RIVER RAT. Flickerings of auburn leaves amass against the river like a stage-set fire. CITY CRUISER eases past. At The Angel a courier in a silver helmet stares out across the river, a black bag of weights slung across a shoulder. Through the estates, to Shad Thames, a beautiful plain girl walks with her mother, under a red umbrella.

CM

8 MARSHALL STREET

We use the steps as a street auditorium
to project poetry, bongo-hassle scaring up 35
there for Niall's coercive raw-fingered chords
working an edgy southern blues for Blake
as a superstring higher-dimensional shape,
he's there as 4 or 5D energy
in orange space-time over Soho.
We nip at a Georgia Moon corn whisky jar
80% moonshine from Tennessee,
the drizzle pixelating glitter puffs
in hazy arcs — Blake's site on Broadwick Street
now a chocolate-fronted Patisserie Valerie,
go round to John Snow's, a Chinese puzzle,
its bitters hoppy as frothed-up Thames spill,
Cherry Fruit Beer, Old Brewery Bitter, Oatmeal Stout,
cloudy as a wonky GABA down-mood.
We're boho hipsters, handgun street poets
pulling the weirdos out of street traffic
to stare a number down where six alleys
network above the squeezed underground chill
of black water. Blake's reconstructed capital
booted investment bankers, hedge funders,
4x4 paramilitary financiers
into the churning sewer at Vauxhall.

We clean the air by giving him back words
as urban rhythm, go off to the pub
cold as the pavement, doing what we do,
standing like gunslingers, back to the wall.

JR

SHAD THAMES REVISITED

I left the Southbank tonight, the sluice dredged back
to the streets of the fruit-barrow metropolis, down
Stamford Street, Southwark Street, the doorsteps of the
cathedral rotten with offerings — black cores, spilt ales —
& onto Tooley Street, past a building called *Sungod*,
the Shipwrights Arms, the bust of Ernest Bevan — his
teacher's crop, the rosebud lips — against the pillbox red
of a bus, & went down to Shad Thames, past the
warehouses replicated in adobe honeycombs, the
bachelor-pad launderettes, larva-lit balconies, a black cab
tanked-out the light on the river & shuddered across
the cambered cobbles, the names writ large — Gabriel's
Wharf, Java, Tea Trade — where I've stood, many times
before, on nights like this, the commuter twilight shot
with purple, ducks slung across the Thames towards
St. Katherine Docks, up the chrome steps I stopped
where the sign said DANGER, NO ADMITTANCE,
listening to the wood slats creak & the green chains
clank at low tide, almost believing that the broken circuit
of the towers at Canary Wharf & the dwarfed clones in
the City were both the same thing : reflected back to
each other in the water.

CM

RED SNAPPER, CECIL COURT

Gun-barrel court off St. Martin's Lane,
Robert Cecil the syphilitic spy's
(1609) — a slab of billionaire high-end
reconstructed West End leaseholds.
We had a shop there run as banditry
for poets, outlaws, dealers, criminals,

tumble-in types like skewed Pete Doherty,
I wrote there all day at a red-slabbed desk
cut like a polished ruby mortuary fridge;
poems I gave away, their energies
like a 747's kerosene spill
cooling after twelve hours of engine thrust.

We took no plastic, only tainted cash,
I remember Pete tipping out notes
dusted with crystals, a crumpled free-fall
like origami fanned out by exhaust
and doing impromptu remakes, the Kinks
worked as a raw submerged 'Waterloo Sunset' drawl…

Aaron kept downstairs, the Soho river
under the floor, a subterranean ooze
deregulated by sharp snappy rains
into a cloudy membrane coating stock,
a low-light lamp on all day, a laptop
pulling books off the net: we worked that way.

We'd sniff the jackals in their Millbank cell
a mile away: brogue-heeled war criminals
brokering spin and burn: you'd get Blair's smell —
lies as they cooked in sticky antigens.
We fuelled the shop on poetry and sounds:
a poem opens into a sunflower

that alters every cell in consciousness.
The bailiffs squeezed us: we survived on style
and luck, sold mostly Bs — Burroughs, Ballard,
the sad, skinny, hippified Brautigan,
and celebrated lawless survival
against liquidation — and lost it all,

eluded seizure, got the stock out fast,
left the landlords a stripped empty shop
and drank at the Salisbury not to an end
but to influence, the lives we'd coloured by
creative space, people who sat on the floor,
read books and came back next day as a friend.

JR

CITY OF LONDON

If we can hear the bells then we take their name,
if it's after The Hour then the bricks are closed,
if it's marked with the Arms we're locked in the centre
— *Lord, direct us* — along Queen Victoria Street,
Distaff Street, Old Fish Street Hill, where
the Walbrook trickles in florins & pence.

The men in luminous direct us upwards
— *Blackfriars Station, Major New Development* —
towards the City of Analogue. A thoroughfare of clocks
hedged with bronze eagles. The white pulse of Canary
Wharf flickers its amphetamine trip-switch but the City's
obelisk-mask has turned the day to stone.

At St Mary Woolnoth there's a Green Man in search
of global beers. THIS SYSTEM IS CONTROLLED
BY PERFECTUS. Staircases off King William Street
lead down past vectors to roofs beneath our feet
— *With a dead sound on the final stroke of nine* —
the river draws me to its future sources in the relics

of the lost — as if the holiday case has sprung & cast
its souvenirs along the A-road to the metropolitan camp.
A half-moon behind The Monument. A Vauxhall stops
and a man in uniform gets out at THE FINE LINE
restaurant. Turn left for DOCKLANDS. A courier
cuts a corner with an L-Plate on his tailpipe,

alert in a blacked-out visor. His sat nav is a clipboard
strung to handlebars & pegged to that : a folio A-Z
of London. His destination circled in HB. The walk
to Tower Bridge captures our shadow twelve times to hard
drive, two of which make laser-jet. Tourists complain
of commuters & talk of the limits of Health & Safety.

Pavements segue to staircase & pull us from the routes
we choose for ourselves, up ramps to roofs
with totem poles that ideogram the seven stages
of man, along a pedestrian runway of white offices
that display perfect desks of stationery but are, for this hour,
closed to us. A turnstile on black space that is locked.

White static runs to the reaches of ceramics & wires
as the river chants its out-takes. Someone has always
been here before : a stone-set foetal head, a clay offering,
is spooling sunlight on the wall of Oliver's warehouse.
Its flippers wind-up static, snout skewed,
eyeholes long bored into cavernous pistol shots.

Its body petrifies on a shingle of corks & clay pipes.
Its dumb weight — hollowed of intestine — trawls centuries
of river-beds. A crab leg pincers beneath a husk of brick —
when I lift that's all there is : a leg punked with fine barbs,
the motion of its amputation pistons towards the shoreline,
claws at the river, wipes without ligament in the breeze.

CM

41

HAM YARD W1

Time-cut 2010: Six months of Wednesday 9.30am hyper-energised photo-shoots slicing time into visual frames, me working exhibitionistically across the derelict piss-drenched 0.75 acre Soho yard for Gregory Hesse's Canon angles; the light sharp like cutting your finger on a tin, or drizzled steamy urban puff. Greg's technology comprised a Canon Ultrasonic 28-200mm, loaded with black and white Ilford HP5 film, 36 exposures, each explosively choreographed shoot, an unrepeatedly interactive 15 minutes leaving both of us emotionally used-up from the intense hit-and-run dynamic.

Our work incentive as Mod aficionados was using me as focus to make a visual document of a cratered yard that housed Ronan O'Rahilly's legendary Scene club, the epicentre of Mod culture in the early 1960s, was accelerated by the news that hotel chain Firmdale, owned by Tim and Kit Kemp, had exchanged contracts to buy Ham Yard for around £30m to build a luxury 100 room hotel, plus 50,000 square feet of housing on an indigenously proto-hipster landmark. To the cooly-dressed, two-tone, tonic-mohair suited Faces or individualists in pilled-up 1964, the site was also known as Pill Yard, due to the gravitation of speed dealers there, selling Drinamyl pills shaped like purple Viagra diamonds both in the yard and inside the 200 capacity Scene club, a blacked-out unlicensed basement on what was a bomb-site back of the Lyric Tavern on Great Windmill Street.

You can't recreate history; it's a series of inaccessible space-times hijacked by imagination, but essentially wiped, like watching the empty grey sky fill in with its floaty cloud architecture after a plane's departed, so Greg and I optimised the acute present with its zillions of localised photons, dodging the XXL waist black sacks for shots fired like a gun with the silencer on.

Ham Yard, which owes its name to a lowlife pub called the Ham in existence there in 1739, and used by robbers and stick up highwaymen, has a defiant counterculture history rooted in music. During the 1920s' fizzy jazz milieu, it was home to the Ham Bone Club for liberated, short-skirted partiers soaking up gin and sexually-charged blues, while in the 1950s, the cellar pioneered Cy Laurie's Skiffle Club, soon to be Cy Laurie's Jazz Basement, a dancing academy during the day, before becoming the seminally cutting-edge druggy Scene club in the 1960s. It was there the likes of The Rolling Stones, The Who, The Pretty Things, The Action and The Animals tore down the walls with their sweaty anarchic volume-up, maximum R&B rip-the-joint dynamic.

The human body is limited by a number of instinctual variant poses, and working within our individual capacities we attempted to intensify rather than diversify a particular look, linking my contorted posture and expressively thrown up arms to the abraded surface of a black peeling wall, a mesh fence post, or simply the menacing atmospherics of a place islanded into residual decay, all DNA traces of customised first-wave Mods rubbed into the yard's gritty dirt.

Time-Cut, the Scene, July 1964: The Jagger phenomenon: 135lbs of skinny dance compression on a compacted 10ft stage, the unlived-in black Anello & Davide Chelsea boots click abrasive castanets, the singer's provocative striptease steps, one foot crossed mincingly over the other in a flurry of yellow nose-coned maracas is so delinquently camp, it's both contagiously arrogant and a punkishly sexualised travesty. He's squeezing raw R&B juice out of the Stones' first full-on unstoppable chart smash, a vandalised speeded-up cover of 'Not Fade Away' that explodes into manic garage, the equivalent of a Ferrari's acceleration from 0-60mph in 3.5 seconds.

He's the look Mods can't fix or dare emulate without being copyist, the sexual ambivalence restructuring the black wool Cecil Gee blazer, three-buttons, waisted, slim lapels, worn insolently over Polo-mint white fly-fronted tab-collar shirt, the figure-forming low-rise silver wool hipsters from John Stephen's His Clothes theming cool with dressy elegance. And for all the intransigent streetwise attitude he projects, the sensibility is one of intelligent remove from the crowd's increasingly liberated hysteria each time he surges into the untutored footwork learnt impromptu from projecting on condensed stages. Jagger's so effortlessly the look, he's creating it so as to be it, hair worn long over the collar and in girlie bangs at the front; Mods won't incorporate him into their aesthetic because to them his look's too accessorised, too individualised a fashion moment. The black painted walls sweat and walk in on the crowd as he squeezes the harmonica to a Jack the Ripper alley wail on 'Confessin' The Blues,' his dance steps choreographing the song's dejected mood-board.

The remaining band members meshed into the flat visceral sound are bleached into off-message insignificance by Jagger's upfront confrontational energies, his physicalised focus of the song becoming its sonic figure so he's its mobility, and the front row dive at his elusive shape-shifting ankles, trying to grab something of him, before a bulky gofer's savvy crunches the offenders back into line.

You can't both *be* him and watch him perform, his vulnerability being sited in his essential passivity — the musical offensive screens his physical fragility; his size-zero androgyny is minded, despite the band's kamikaze rip each time they come on in a policed precinct to tear it up with insurgent bad-boy blues lifted from black.

Jagger's Scene club reinventions are like Dilly rent around the corner — a transgressive fact you fixate on to lose, because he's so far ahead of gender preconceptions, he's always going to win. When he's gone the floor's littered with pills, cans, the fretwork graffiti nailed by his Cuban heels. A girl's crying by the exit, another's slashed her number in red lipstick on the wall. It's over, 30 imperiously burnt-out tribal Stones minutes — the Jagger phenomenon — Mississippi Delta impersonator in clothes you'd die for. Outside it rains; the yard rinsed by the percussive shower that drenches fans running all the way to the tube at Piccadilly Circus to go under in 1964: a busy slice of time programmed into two-minute pop songs — 'Not Fade Away' (Petty/Hardin), and accelerating towards the end of time in the cosmic microwave background radiation.

Time Cut 2010: After the shoot Greg and I go review a printed wallet of black and white photos from the previous week at Bar Bruno, an unpretentious, hyperactive native Soho café on the junction of Peter Street and Wardour Street and chill over mint tea in the conversationally-loud greasy spoon ambience. I tell Greg how I find myself often squatting down, compelled to make contact with the yard's fissured asphalt surface, as though looking for signs to the place written into its compacted urban dirt, like micro-fault lines. There's a cyan arrow and serial number demonstrably painted there as part of the Thames blue ribbon network.

On one occasion I bought a bunch of dark red M&S roses to the shoot; we called it the Ham Yard funeral session and left the roses bang up against a boarded window of the black flaking façade that was the Scene as a gesture of improvised street glamour. Each shoot was an affirmative last stand, a retrieval of a soon-to-be submerged space by two thin interactive figures ritualising place: nowhere to run and 500 exposures bringing it all defiantly home.

JR

Alderman Stairs, E1

Under Alderman Stairs chains latch
to brick, moss-covered steering wheels
of Volvos silenced in the woods
— interiors hushed with vines —
an anchor rigged with a rope of horsehair
and matted with sponge. The city's
urgencies close-off above, quaint
as tea-rooms from the debris & crush
of this basement shoreline, a cellar
of thanatos drinking games. A shingle
of dud electrics glint the base of a glass
like a monocle that blinds, the petrified
crust of a stout bottle holograms
an eagle in the tide's dispensary — we drink
to ooze these toxins merrily. What sunlight
the city takes in early March is caged here,
like the underside of a disused pier, ribbed
with blackened timber & splintered barge-
beds. I walk like a hangman that scattered
the revellers as the grey beach rolls
under my treads on an axis of lichen —
finger-nails hook damp wood for gravity.
A trickle like coins from a hostelier's
pouch counts itself in crustaceous syllables
from under the stairs : there, like a kissing
chamber enclosed in the corner, a stream
runs from a lost river or a leak from
an ancient watermain, choking back
to its source. My shadow sprawls on the

bricks beneath, as if to attach itself to itself
and multiply under stalactites in this unit
of storage the city fails to lease, a hub for
rats & disused fibre-optics. There is enough
space to sit inside & for the river to rise
and cancel this bucket of oxygen, closing
London back to ground level as the detritus
swirls to the surface for the tea-drinkers
to watch — swirls of champagne corks,
consumables — that submerge again & rise
with the broken glass & the bladderwrack.

CM

Mods, Hoodlums, Guttersnipes, Punks

He's that skinny, 26" waist Mark Feld, aka Marc Bolan, proto-glam cool hanging out in Soho's unreconstructed sixties teen wasteland, in dodgy red-light drizzled reefer-pungent Archer Street, selling sex at the Dilly to maintain his Mod look as a Stamford Hill polymorphic pop wannabe. At a pretty dandified maladjusted fourteen, he tells *Town* magazine that his maverick wardrobe comprises "ten suits, eight sports jackets, fifteen pairs of slacks, thirty or thirty-five good shirts, about twenty jumpers, three leather jackets, two suede jackets, five or six pairs of shoes and thirty exceptional ties." His distinctly negotiable Cockney identity fused to a hustling sexual ambiguity — his clothes undoubtedly pulled from the slippery readies deposited always after earning, under your feet between sock and shoe-sole at the Piccadilly meat-rack, or under the street on the station's circular concourse monitored by assiduously energised police surveillance. His voice a quivering barrow boy's monotone bongoed into a lisping mantra; was that the same voice he employed coercively and defensively in his fast uptake exchange with predatory Dilly punters, or was it camper, more like a girl's voice bruised by testosterone, but savvy, Cockney, don't-mess-with-me-mister, rechargeable? What he picked up was Tyrannosaurus Rex, an acoustic two-piece featuring his bongo-playing partner Steve Peregrine Took, his voice converted into a stuttering, mumbled register, a monochromatic often inarticulate chant; the lyric submerged by affected delivery, a style clearly adopted by rent, where a non-committal answer, sometimes in the gay slang called Polari, is left questionably hanging in disconnect as a preliminary to sussing-out whether someone is a genuine punter or insidious plain-clothes police. Bolan's vocal technique was learnt there on the commercialised meniscus of a smoke-and-mirrors W1 pavement, a site where anyone standing still in the transient accelerated foot-traffic focused into work, travel or recreation, is arguably selling or buying sex in Bolan's lugubrious rent ethos.

> He's bona vada
> in bitchy mascara
> selling for metzers
> to buy nanna pizza
> a blowjob buys hipsters
> or slinky black leather
> he's been eating dead babies
> > a red fabu Max Factor

and runs into David Jones, aka Bowie, a south Brixton copyist, entrepreneurially trawling Wardour Street for breaks, a tarted-up Mod-inflected guttersnipe with an eclectic taste for showbiz artifice, equally sexually ambivalent, and hanging out as a prescient ingénue at smoky rooms like the Giaconda in Denmark Street, Les Enfants Terrible in Dean Street, the rent-patronised La Macabre in Meard Street, La Bastille on Wardour Street, lowlife Soho cafes amalgamating musicians, writers, working girls, sharp-suited gangsters into an iconoclastic sixties nougat, pitted with rhinestones and paste, a chewy malleable texture into which Bowie was stuck. 'London Boys' was his autobiographical attempt to condense his Soho experience; from an unmanageably shape-shifting artist without a focused genre into a hustling pilled-up Mod desperado, who gets drugs, despondency, and into Wardour Street, with variant piss tangs, champagne, wine, methadone and beer, all ventricularly networked into yards.

Bowie's looking for the quantum wave-form piggyback to Ziggy that he still hasn't found, because he hasn't yet learnt how to hijack a persona and project it like cosmic wormholing into a short cut. He's got a cigar box full of slap and makeup, a pocket full of speed and he and Bolan lift their stage clothes from the shop rejects in Carnaby Street black sacks on Saturday nights, reconstructing rejects with a zip out, an unstitched seam, a partially invisible snick in a pink cashmere V-neck to be ingeniously made-over with a sewing machine. Bowie's gone bottle-blond, soaking up faggy, light-polluted foodie-orientated Wardour Street, and going back nights to live with his gay manager Ken Pitt in Manchester Street in a dope fog swirling into a reeking mandala.

> You're daddy I'm chicken
> connie's delish
> you're a bum pusher buffet
> I'm zhooshy on hashish
> vada well zhooshed riah
> you'll tip the velvet
> I dunno if I'ze queer
> > I wanna rock permit

Someone's metabolised the capital's everyday ambience like a monolithic 659-square-mile pill, assimilated its everyday places and experiences into songs begun up high on a broken sofa. Summited above the city at Muswell Hill, Ray Davies literally writing down through floating clouds, off-white alto-cirrus, into the city, and down through Highgate into the commercialised West End; Ray stabbing maniacally at a piano for the storyline for his brother Dave's subversive three-chord fuzz-box guitar that's a shattering subversive first — 'You Really Got Me,' like you can never again extract the sound from your hypothalamus after it's stimulated the right amygdala into overdrive. The dandified, villagey brothers do London songs, river indigenous as pie and mash, urban gritty as falling in love under a tomato-red traffic light — Ray's brokering what Bolan and Bowie can't, urban micro-novels with characterisation, 'Dedicated Follower of Fashion,' 'Dead End Street' and the seminally elegiac 'Waterloo Sunset', a rusty-flavoured song, as though the lyric is bolted together by oxidized nuts like the infrastructural metalwork of Waterloo Station. Ray's partially sardonic nonchalance — he's a misanthropic romantic — is exploded by Dave's guitar, slashing at the lyrics like an insurgent carjacker blading cellulose. 'Waterloo Sunset's the protein building-blocks of most London pop, it's an eroded slab with irregular windows most bands memory-check or run up against as referential pop architecture you can't get around. Ray's a sensitive hoodlum with an ear for the capital's dialectic like the variant mix of colours in the river's churned up mood-board under Waterloo. He's the off-mood raconteur you'll never properly pin, the edgy depressant in velvet foppery, and the songs are the lyrical resources of an essentially dystopian vision of the capital and its homogenised invasion of local.

Go under the street, the stripped-down 100 Club on Oxford Street, beneath the old straight track that led to Tyburn's gallows at Marble Arch, sited on blood and the full-on carbon-polluted red sun that faces down on the incessant corridor of foot traffic like streaming live video. A stain that's neon-red, vermilion, crimson, ox-blood, maroon, crushed fig, plasma/haemoglobin. Johnny's there, the naff leering criminal Lydon, a Small Faces wannabe a decade too late, voice like a marketer's put through a parmesan grater, but for all the aggro vulnerable, a music-hall punk romantic backed by bandits. They use industrial cleaner on the Small Faces' 'Watcha Gonna Do About It', changing the lyric from "I love you" to "I hate you" — sneering contempt, and Johnny periodically blows his nose on stage out of boredom; that voice come out of the choked Thames blue ribbon network — "Gimme a fakkin drink. Pleeeeze." The Pistols are spike-haired discharged Mafia, heroin veterans disrupting all notion of chords in their catastrophic rip of sound into air-crash free-fall through the speakers. Lydon's so hard, so compressed on the vocal, the song goes into anti-boredom rocket rejection phase at two minutes. Skinny ties, narrow collars, second-hand bondage trousers, messed angular hair — you get 'Anarchy in the UK,' and 'God Save the Queen' as kerosene no-music, a dramatic rupture with rock's past delivered with abrupt handgun shots. Wannabe Krays on at the Blind Beggar.

JR

EUSTON

Euston — the enforcer —
black powerplant on the hill
overlooking the hospital.
In the soot of the rain,
midwinter, we stood on
Southampton Row :
a family with no outward passes.
Thousands passed without faces,
collars & hats — anonymous —
umbrellas webbed in carapace.
The enforcer's gross structures
obliterate millimetres;
inside the boy were byways & blockages
the city had no surveillance on;
gross hydronephrosis of kidneys,
ureter implanted to the surface,
the surgeon's dexterity in weaving
flesh for love. The anonymous
in thousands above Victorian
water-mains, abandoned stations,
a city beneath of rats & infestations.
The enforcer's red guards
pumped the fearless in enclosed cells
to Nuneaton, Watford, Holyhead,
ours the only faces exposed, identities known,
admin logged for the surgeon's 4am call :
Euston the one way outwards.
The enforcer had shredded
all outward passes.

CM

HERON TOWER

Sea-green Starbucks cardboard wrapper
as hot finger stops on a paper cup
sipped on a street chair facing Heron Tower's
46 storeys — clear reflective glass
like a hologrammed vertical coffin —
a hedge-funders' quantum demographic
selling futures in sealed silver foils
like a lubed aqua micro-thin condom
rolled on a brokered configuration
aimed like the tower's double deck high-speed lifts
surging 203 metres to the stratospheric sky bar.
What does a poem weigh against cladded steel
costing £242m? My image bank's
resources fire-up neural weaponry
like cyber-battle. Everywhere I hear
water shaking hands underground, a stream
lacing another like two black silk ties
doing a tango in a dodgy pipe.
I write the tower into my poetry —
Kohn Pedersen Fox: white mast in the clouds,
their idea came weightlessly digitised,
the first thought lighter than the last —
I call it architectural calories.
I face its intelligent solar shield's
photovoltaic cells, an E1 transplant brain
sited in Bishopsgate, a part of me: the city's pull
into my gut, having me hang out there,
just sighting what I do; constructing words
out of carbon-based chemistry.

JR

THE THAMES PATH

is a fallacy, a disturbance of stone sections stuttering
the flow of the Thames — through hotel foyers, car parks,
beer & public gardens, past kitchen vents, monuments,
under bridges, and when it breaks — between Broken
Wharf and Queenhithe — past a *Fitness First* & a flock of
parked scooters like gulls broken with corrugation you
see the path for what it is : a creation myth for the sale
of leisure, a crippled thoroughfare of urban build latched
at late-notice against the river, as the grebe tucks itself
under the waves — its neck wrapped under its breast like
a birthing glove — the bricks display their own principles
of memory — layers scarred with cavities — the bunkers
dug, filled & built upwards : on nights like this I've
watched the shopping complex of Surrey Quays take its
customers like passengers down the decks of aisles &
issue them like stevedores packing their own ashes.

CM

SHOPLIFTING AT SELFRIDGES

My thin friend looks exo-planetary,
the off-world type dressed cool by Richard James,
blue space in his eyes like the China Sea

and dodgy like he counted sugar grains
as focus, filtering them into tea.
He tells me nicking's extrasensory,

dark matter glues galaxies together
and what you pull from jumper stacks instore's
third in the pile, or straight off the counter,

what the left eye attracts by looking right.
He recommends do small talk, make things float,
de-tag with a hook piece, his slippery tricks —

and sometimes uses a detacher gun.
A habituated forensic pro,
he looks money, but needs dopamine kicks.

In the black-marbled Selfridges slab,
an art deco commercialised sarcophagus,
he robs like a retail shrinkage bandit:

his thrill's accelerated by the lights,
their drizzled starburst dazzle when he's on,
brain chemicals car-chasing what he sights —

a striped Westwood cardie done as a trick
that dematerialises instantly.
I got that one: he steals to give away

like my best scent, Vetiver by Guerlain.
He's Nick, and even blocked on Naltrexone
can't help it, always that compulsive grab

to subvert order, leave the pile deplete
like it's numerical, odd not even,
and goes off doing numbers down Duke Street.

JR

DOCKLANDS, THAT TORY CREATION

Find your own path from Southwark to Brunel.
On London Bridge, under the *Pie & Ale* sign,
the clock is still stuck at twenty-to-twelve; the 141
steers its vessel through black puddles & passengers
watch the feet of walkers numbly hunt the pavements,
— each step a crusade for leisure destinations —
the rabies-foam of oil & mud froths up the flags
from beneath their treads, a white pigeon takes flight
over Tooley Street in its self-concept of dove
— a fan in flames — & flies over the tiles of old hostelries.
In the doorways of The Pommelers, Sunday drinkers smoke
staring up the stone thorax of Tower Bridge
to the base of Lower Thames Street & consider movement
across to *The Little Ship Club* & the Custom House —
abandoned warehouses, strolling arcades,
through the plug-and-play of glass domes
and the warning *Walkway subject to occasional floods*,
the modular addition to the Tower of London
with the rewrite of INFORMATION as SHOP,
the Monument buses' enamel pillboxes, windows
shedding flat parcels of April light,
past the City Cruises & Thames Clippers, the Queen's Stairs
studded with latches & spigots — ice-cream vans
revving internal grilles — caramel nutmen in chainmail
dry-frying their ware, through Dead Man's Hole landmarked
with a bile-black oval to the pooled courtyards of Ivory House,
International House, Tower Hotel, Commodity Quay,
where the lichen huts trade tartan cardigans : this is where
the Apartment Trolls reside, their genitals spiteful anemones,
each buttock tanked with cellulite. When Heseltine looked down

from his jet through the patch on his eye & saw the centuries
of decay alchemise into a development called *Docklands*
he had no idea that Mellor would buy the Dockmaster's House
and market these heroics in paid-for sex in a Chelsea kit
— the Apartment Troll, hedge-fund Caliban —
obstructing the build of a high-rise in his own backyard.

CM

Norton Folgate

Dick stick-up Turpin's parish, bandit dude,
no plastic, only bling and flash,
a leather wristlock grabbing cash,
a gun snouting the carotid's
blipping quasar, he'd strip them nude

if they resisted force. On Folgate Street
the light arriving seems to stay
like time-cutting video:
are the photons full of spatial info
the same dusty ones I saw yesterday

as gold-polluted dazzle, carbon haze?
Dick sniffs for J.P. Morgan, stiffs
investment bankers, wears a black eye-patch
and rips them like a virtual alligator
or a Tornado GR4

nuking a shelled Libyan tank.
Dick's the beef in Bishopsgate,
his fat cat's cock turns gold in Blossom Street
slashing metabolised profits at a wall
hallucinating 1739

rope-burn cutting into his twisted neck
hoisted to the mobster Tyburn gallows,
the crowd big as an O2 revival gig,
his loot stashed away like WMD,
the thing like a psychotic episode

only it's happening. He lopes
into the Water Poet for troubleshooters,
the black pavement grid outside rumbling streams
as the city's diagnostic read-out
of its bacterial anthology.

His dealing room's his killing field;
spread-betting while thunder slams in
as fizzy atmospheric dialect,
a black slash over Spital Square,
breaking that moment into violent rain.

JR

THE CHELSEA OF WILDE & THATCHER

A seaside of the North pitches-up on the Thames
and they rise from the shallows against MI6 :
squid-white cockle-pickers of information. Chelsea
is space as the City is time. Battersea exists
for perspective with an obsolete bandstand silenced
to pagoda. The skyline broadens to rivet all possibles.
Wilde lived twice on Tite Street, the first was this :
THE RIVER HOUSE, flagged by a lamp-post's tag —
Do not dig within two metres of this mast.
Every view of Chelsea is a vista of weathercocks.
No. 46, THE TOWER HOUSE, declares its frame
for the people with the authority to make namings.
Property-nomenclature. No. 34 remains un-named
but marks its ghost by blue plaque : OSCAR WILDE
1854-1900 WIT AND DRAMATIST LIVED HERE.
Symbolist Poet in relegation from the language arts.
A balcony terrace above, basement flat beneath,
before me a locked wooden box glossed in emulsion.
Over the trestle-terrace & fin-de-siècle masonry
a room of March sun from Dorian's genesis
*there is such a little time that your youth will last—
such a little time.* Behind me Audi keys chink
and a daughter hugs her mother & they both say
I love you as if trying to steal each other's PIN.
I follow the self-locking coal-holes onto Redburn
Street like stone-set commemorative coins —
until my breath catches — this is where she lived —
the burn in the diaphragm ignites on Flood Street.
Codified now with the outposts of the underclass —
a Young's Pub & a William Hill. The bookmakers
smells of potpourri as the commentary soundbleeds

the pavements : *Camden George is coming up on*
the rail, the outsider, taking on Copper's Gold…
the Iron Lady lived outside the river's drowning urge,
King's Road end, where men walk slow-pace & prompt
conversations with *I can't believe….*THE HALL
OF REMEMBRANCE opposite, does, in fact, work :
an image of my dad rigging a fix-lock on the gas
to alter the rates in the same year as the Poll Tax.
No. 19 : where she stood with a sweep after succeeding
Heath (my dad worked seven days & said, before he
died, he'd missed us growing up); No. 19 : the venue
for the meeting of her first shadow cabinet (later,
his Saturdays at home, my mum passed us like shadows
to work lotteries). No. 19 : the trestles are tangled
in creepers & the scaffolding to the roof crabbed
in vines. Behind, a convertible hosting a picnic quest
— a hedge-fund *Wind in the Willows* cast —
tries to reverse to let the tarred kneecap of a hackney past.
The cars behind flex in support
and a chain-lock of shouts ripple
across Range Rover, Porsche, Lexus, Jag…
Two of the men in collar-check shirts open the doors
and emerge from the mental-scrum of public schools :
the cabbie, a bigger man, road-checks with size & they
both back off. But it's a resolution of necessity :
the cabbie's got to work, his meter's attached to the rates
he pays. He reverses back into the King's Road
and the cavalcade of beeswax rolls away from view.

Bladder flicks a blade in consciousness. I size-up
the Lady's baize-green door. The coward does it with
a kiss, the brave man with a sword. Don't fancy either.
Put back thy cock. No milk-snatcher's worth your piss.

CM

64

THE RIGHT HON. JACKAL BLAIR

Insensitive as a mortuary fridge,
a jackal's
asymmetrically psychopathic grin
like killing's chutzpah, meltdown's fun
people stick like eggs to a pan

fried by depleted uranium
under a radioactive desert sun
neon-red as a traffic light.
Blair's the hipster-suited super-killer
the cool czar monetising war

into personalised futures capital.
The burnt, the mutilated don't move now,
nor bacon-rashered Iraq amputees.
The J.P. Morgan commissar's slap's
a flakeover fake tan

sealing his features when he lies
into a harassed orange smear.
He throws handgun body shapes, sticky spin,
like the man who blew up the world
as missile-guided music hall.

The guilt lodged like a bullet in his brain
he can't extract, a toxic leak
like slow-dose polonium.
His look's impassive as an army truck
an explosive self-propelled howitzer.

He's aggro sicko psycho
a blacked-out Range Rover his cell
locked into minders like a gang
of decommissioned brick-faced commandos
maintaining a globe-trotting criminal.

JR

Rotherhithe

St. Quays Court to Neptune Street, across
St. George's fields to the Dock Offices
and found the blue plaque : ON SEPTEMBER 7
1940 THIS SITE WAS SET ON FIRE IN THE FIRST
BLITZ TO HIT LONDON. Inside cranial ovals
gnaw on BICs, an inheritance shadowed with ink.
If I was to count my face amongst theirs
— on the outside of the glass, pressing HB to card —
what will our system be, how in the sediment
layers of the docks will we find this moment again?
Down in the tide's bracken borsch I make an index
fathomed in five-bar gates of barcodes shredded
from plastics, a rucksack smorgasbord of pines
and flints, a log piked in black strikes, bottle tops,
straws, tobacco packs, nutritional information
flaked from attachments — a potpourri of river-
dredge — & further east a red rose
stapled to moss laminates an obituary:
IN MEMORY OF PATRICK (PAT) PRICE 17/3/1935 —
22/1/1995 WHO USED TO SWIM AND PLAY
FROM BUTLER'S WHARF AS A CHILD WHILE HIS
DAD WORKED THE CRANES FROM THIS SPOT.

Childhoods of chrome that have rusted in love,
calcified in encodings of date & name & place.
Passers-by watch as I'm writing this — & I add them in —
filed under Human Remittances.

CM

LONDON FLOWERS

These oriental poppies earthed
as scattered outtakes, rough demos
lucked into NW3
shivery silk minis on runway pins —
pink, yellow, orange, blue and red,
they're like randomised confetti
transient saucerians
an anthology of MAC eye colours
in nitrogen-depleted soil.
I give them names like Toyoko,
Masako, Yumiko, O,
Yuan Yuan, a garden harem
cooking Chinese opium.
Ixia and violet iris
lyricise intense moments,
so too explosive azaleas
and a libidinous steamy lily,
a transplant brain from Asia
with a bulb like a shaved cortex.
This marine blue hydrangea's
the colour of the blue deodorant cube
floating in the Gatwick men's toilet,
a sort of deep Atlantic blue
squirted with ultramarine.
Like everything I see they're poetry,
poppies bringing a dusty frill
to capital affairs, a bright
liaison like a thought pattern;
immediate as light checked-in

8 mins travel time from the sun
to reach this wiry leggy cluster
that tomorrow will be gone.

JR

St Saviour's Dock, Bermondsey

but on those same winter nights I would walk down to
St. Saviour's Dock when the tide was out, the basin
drained back to its source & be shook by how — amongst
the splintered barks of wood & sludge — there was always
a mattress slumped across the mud — buckets, packets,
tickets — the remains of what had drifted from balconies,
the refuse of conversion-living, the barred windows open
to expose the bricks back to the North Sea's dispensation
of semtex & plastics. If you'd have stood where I stood,
that winter night, watching the City's exposed SIMs falter
towards Canary Wharf, BT Tower's revolving needle,
the docks — St Katherine, Shadwell — Canada Square's
charged prongs like a cross-section of Manhattan skyline,
a latchkey of hyper-communications cut-out against the
reaches of the marshes, exposing the peninsula of the
People's Republic as a moat of duff consensus, & watched
the wood turrets of the Thames opposite Tate — down
to Broken Wharf & Queenhithe — you'd know the Victorian
barge-beds once used for vessels to land off-shore,
splintered & swollen & loose in the sand, the river
absolving the shards in caressing Os, long after the spices
& teas have ceased to arrive, exposed as perches for the
black & white checkmate of the cormorants and gulls — a
wellington, a torn boot — mould spores clinging to their
soles — you'd have turned back for home questioning as I
did : where the river's drive for commerce failed & where
the tapering for the stars will end.

CM

KIT MARLOWE

The tattooed boozed-up brawler on Hog Lane,
knuckles slashed to ketchup dollops,
fighting at knife-point in rain's
persistent steamy shattering:
"You're paid by fucking Shakespeare, man,"
he screams, and his friend cuts the boy
over a rumbling Holborn drain
popping with oozy black diamonds.
Kit's the pub hustler, gangsta grime
mixed in with poetry like uncut jewels,
his eloquent line like a gangland raid.
"You tell that motherfucker queer
I'll run him through next time he tries
to have me sprung — you got it clear?"
They leave him ear split open like a fig.
He's lowlife Shoreditch Christofer Marley,
money-laundering gay defiant punk
trawling the bars, a spy for draggy class
in ostrich feathers. A black sailor inks his tattoos
at foggy Limehouse docks: a green dragon
spitting out violet stars. It's 1592:
the city's tang is piss, the river tugs
the drowned into a missing persons' heap.
Kit's back in London 2002
tracking Blair's sex-up spin-buddy raw Alistair,
hacking his phone: the river's moody blue
dissolving emeralds: the toxic debt
accumulative as bad cholesterol.
He hacks Whitehall: his name still sticks to books
as bad reminders, stuff he can't let go.

JR

BATTERSEA

A policeman stoops over a mini *A-Z*,
holds it like a prayer book – trees from St. Thomas'
corrugate the wall, tin chutes of sewerage
pumped post-procedures – wardens, support
officers, shell-spooks mutter in lapels,
across the shore I count each husk & carapace
as the geese move like tyre tracks
indecipherable in the sludge. The Power Station
rises, ministry of vanished plumes,
cathedral of echoes, its four confessionals
amplified to funnels, air-built barge-beds
for the dreadnought of the clouds. It spreads
its Versailles over Battersea as the circus
camps in its reaches, a carousel of multiplex
retails outlets, the last dock cranes rusted
to heritage. Your last thoughts will not be in words
but in the details of the landscape you lived your life
beneath; will be the points the architects scored
the skyline with. But the river's for the living :
gated with spikes & clovered with mildew & moss
the Thames here is closed to us. The refrain of the siren reads :
PARKS   POLICE   NOTICE   NO   BBQs
and   AFFORDABLE   ART   FAIR (UNDER £3000)
and glyphed to pavement the directions that pull
and stretch the sinew-cords of our senses, that run
coloured chalks in codes of bureaucratic languages

A metal pin scores the centre. On Grosvenor Road
I pick up a cheque from a puddle left blank to the stars
and in this poem make its deposit.

CM

SEVEN DIALS

The granite needle's plinth is the place I chill,
seven roads: and a hot pink Gorgeous Flowers
Vauxhall Vivaro G106 GIG offloads
on Earlham Street. Got my materials,
Silvine Student's Notebook Red Code 141
A4 Side Wirokraft Notebook

5055133 184863
barcodes like brand logos are poetry,
the coded chromosomal bits
to lyric pops. What's bluer than blue air —
Urban Decay's Dashiki eyeshadow
and cool as patenting a gene,

an uploaded Michael Jackson cell line
estimate ten billion dollars.
Thom Neal's 1692 six roads,
one square's under green sheeted scaffolding,
a reconstruction project. When we meet
(Caffe Nero) you give me Tom Clark's *Stones*

Harper & Row 1969, jacket
a Joe Brainard black spotty affair on yellow,
the time-cut's just like wave function,
a quantum rehab. Slice through any day
it's like a sci-fi lemon drizzle cake.
Joe's dead: we're there by Short's Gardens

junction of Monmouth Street, London by default.
If we died on the street, left to decay,
would rot be faster than a pizza box
or open jar of mayonnaise
or rogue radioisotope?
We're a mismatched global academy

at this dysfunctional take-no-prisoners site.
I use the way the city uses me
indifferently — we lose in giving lose
defiantly — I'd like to write it down
over and over what I've lost and won
in every poem fired-up in this town.

JR

WHAT THE COURIER KNOWS

3,011 interpreters along Whitehall

20,586 translators in The City

152 actuaries on the short stretch of Norton Folgate

12,701 code-makers for bank credits in Shoreditch

1,298,402 serotonin uplifters port-holed in blister-packs

312 languages in one metropolis, owners of numerical systems & job descriptions

98,919 strip-owners of Visa in Chelsea

156,983 signature scrawls across unsecured cheques in Southwark

102,101 Blackberries like handheld cabs across Docklands

50,241 underarm toxins on Commercial Road

11,001 hotel swipe-cards in Bloomsbury

34,789 coiled ring-pulls on the Isle of Dogs

27,703 ex-east-enders in Dagenham

3,412 SIM cards plasticised inside Canary Wharf

742 new fragments of poetry on notebooks across 33 boroughs

8,041 units of ethanol consumed on Charing X Road

604 obsolete graffitoes on the Old Kent Road

30,312 minutes of conversation exchanged for billed tariff on Denmark Street (*I love you* spoken 989 times)

401 therapists in Golders Green

748,060,099 bones of the non-living weaving the Thames shoreline

312 languages, tongues like skinned dogs

CM

LAMBETH BRIDGE

The river's grey brain-matter over green
a shimmied tidal hypothalamus
dumping on crunchy shingle, slowed-up drag
under pixelating September drizzle.
If I had a microphone
I'd hear the river's heartbeat, double bass
descending to zero
up Lambeth way. I've come from Bill's
(Bill Franks), a personal seminal fashion hero
floored second-floor at Peninsula Heights,
you sight the river below like a pool
green as a cat's eye shot hazel.
I do a valium to up the scene;
see green-grey as more swirly optimal
on 10mgs benzo efficacy.
A sighting cormorant monitors the beach —
a T-bar head on a black umbrella,
close up a sheeny bottle green —
and repositions downriver in puddled slosh.
I've left the arches for the Whitehall side,
the oligarchs and spin who've rocked the world
into catastrophic black gold meltdown.
I take a back route to avoid their black-hole pull
into plotting World War Three,
but keep the river in me and its speed
fine-tuned inside my arteries,
and know Bill catches it from his window,
the pick-up rhythm as the tide restarts
the stick change of its continuous flow.

JR

Peckham Rye (Hymn for Blake)

February 8 : Levi banshee with cheek-scarf & iPod. No. 63.
7:48 am. NO VISION.

February 13 : dreadnought Sunday, chalk-flecks of commuters.
No. 63. 7:32 am. NO VISION.

February 18 : white Mac motherboard reboot, joggers like
data-strings. No. 12. 7:02 am. NO VISION.

February 19 : concentrics of rain in puddles as if Scientologists'
little gods are sticklebacks. No. 63. 8:12 am. NO VISION.

March 3 : cold worming the marrow, no. 13 stranded towards
Elephant & Castle. No. 12. 8:07 am. NO VISION.

March 8 : a crow hawks its quota of dough into the moment
of daffodils. No. 63. 8:58 am. NO VISION.

March 13 : crows dance like henchmen frogging a maypole.
No. 12. 8:19 am. NO VISION.

March 17 : arctic furnace of tin daffodils, a love-locket of
silver Volvos. No. 63. 7:43 am. NO VISION.

March 27 : laminated sheet stapled to moss, *Dear friend,
acknowledge the word of the Lord & believe it : it is truth.*
Starlings like wooden tops. No. 12. 8:48 am. NO VISION.

April 6 : the Winter's last sputum gullies to tissue & is
wrapped like dim-sum. No. 63. 8:23 am. NO VISION.

April 23 : O God let it break now   this blister-

Sundays & if it can't be   like
from the clods   of his feet to the
alloys   of angelic wings &
                                            father for
                                                    li

then let
from the strap
& if not a VISION
the seraphim of endorphins

                                            for which I

pack of self in the   month of premature

Blake's   a boy of ten looking up
boughs spangled   with the Atlantic
if the beating that waits   as his from a
fact-making
 es

                                     it not be
                                 of my own flesh
                               a display at least of
                            from myself to myself

give thanks

                                              CM

DEATH TANGO

Chatterton buys arsenic, atomic number 33, (a dark
   thundery grey)
24.8.1770, his ripped blue military greatcoat
pockets out, popped gilt buttons, pre-punk deconstructed,
   broken, hungry, fixated
on death back of Holborn, Shoe Lane Workhouse,
     it's you
     Tommy who
     watcha gonna do
     do baby blue

Blake tags London with hallucinated graffiti
his urine's like a psychedelic rainbow
slashed on Broadwick Street — a psychotropic uric smear
     I pick off writing on his steps
in drizzle, Soho smudge, tea in a branded paper cup,
   Patisserie Valerie:
     It's you
     Billy who
     watcha gonna do
     do baby blue

Pete, with your green banjo case, dandified mister Doherty
your writing's coagulated with crimson blood,
plasma and haemoglobin in the text
     the way ink bites — it's Whitechapel Chinese rocks
metabolised into streetwise poetry
     it's you
     Peter who
     watcha gonna do
     do baby blue

Johnny, I found you hurt in Soho so
alone, writing was your one way to mend
the homeless blues like Tommy's blue poison
        Chatterton's scorched viscera: you and me
we don't know that we do it (poetry)
        it's you
        Johnny who
        watcha gonna do
        do baby blue

Jeremy, poetry's your death tango
cellular addiction (dopamine receptors)
the moment turns on language that the street deletes
        you'll die wearing a black highwayman's coat
a repro, pills to OD as a last saliva tango
        it's you
        Jeremy who
        watcha gonna do
        do baby blue

JR

INFRA: Cherry Garden Pier

for Tom Chivers

Tom likes his mudlarks with dogs' teeth & electrics.

He larks in the mud for fin-de-siècle ceramics glyphed WAP.

In a wireless sense he wants a ROT at Rotherhithe.

Every mudlark must have an anchor-rope for the
    heart's envelope.

Tom has two alarms : one in new technology & another to
    sleep through.

He fingers the quilled quiff of a gull feather that you would
    never touch.

A lover's totem curse is saved to roach the fragments of
    Victorian clay pipes.

Earthenware is the too-dry crust that the Thames vomits back.

Tom's kingfisher Nikon & silverfish Samsung have nothing
    on them

of nappy-green sludge, though
centuries from this
in the new ceramics
we'll find our place
in the dry wash
of nano-drives
and SIM cards,
the clues to us
unindexed
in online graves.

Hours later, watching the tide from across the river
two licensed frauds hover with metal detectors
to make some kind of living from this —

Tom has our mudlarks embossed in live script

INFRA : spooked.
INFRA : commuters.

INFRA : each sample
pending its end
result.

INFRA : aquifers.
INFRA : fragment.

INFRA : pending catastrophe
in everything you
never said.

INFRA : adrenalin.
INFRA : flint.

INFRA : happiness we're
self-promised
pending.

INFRA : uranium.
INFRA : SIM.

INFRA : date pending
your diary's turn
we never kept.

INFRA : bacteria.
INFRA : methadone.

INFRA : one medication
mistook for another
to no effect.

INFRA : Martian.
INFRA : surveillance.

INFRA : you keep calling
me up to your
basement.

INFRA : warehouse.
INFRA : grilles.

INFRA : sometimes I miss
the person I could
have been.

INFRA : completion.
INFRA : project.

INFRA : with a physique
like this why leave
the mind behind?

INFRA : Pentel.
INFRA : static.

INFRA : don't put the
danger sign in
your mouth.

INFRA : Burroughs.
INFRA : Shad.

INFRA : this relationship
and credit are such
precious things.

INFRA : hedge funds.
INFRA : Shard.

INFRA : body to die for
is no longer a figure
of speech.

INFRA : Jagger.
INFRA : Brunel.

INFRA : original is only
best if it makes you
feel like this.

INFRA : pharmaceutical.
INFRA : thanatos.

INFRA : I don't hail the
same light as every
one else.

INFRA : polymorphic.
INFRA : enforcer.

INFRA : conventional form
is a subversion
of linkage.

INFRA : hologrammed.
INFRA : wharf.

INFRA : taking away from no
thing this removal of
emptiness.

INFRA : Naltrexone.
INFRA : toxins.

INFRA : good sensation every
one & welcome
to today.

INFRA : bacterial.
INFRA : Lexus.

INFRA : the ashtray's grammar
after our breath ceased
in smoke.

INFRA : polonium.
INFRA : remittances.

INFRA : black ice, no mix —
this cocktail of
difficulties.

INFRA : transient.
INFRA : semtex.

INFRA : you keep calling
me up to your
basement.

INFRA : Shoreditch.
INFRA : dreadnought.

INFRA : each sample
pending its end
result.

INFRA : Brainard.
INFRA : courier.

INFRA : happiness we're
self-promised
pending.

INFRA : quantum.
INFRA : Docks.

INFRA : I don't hail the
same light as every
one else.

INFRA : Benzo
INFRA : Blake.

INFRA : this relationship
and credit are such
precious things.

INFRA: Chatterton.
INFRA: Xeroxed.

INFRA : you keep calling
me up to your
basement.

INFRA: adrenalin.
INFRA: SIM.

INFRA: Burroughs.
INFRA: Shard.

INFRA: transient.
INFRA: wharf.

INFRA: quantum.
INFRA: Blake.

INFRA : INFRA : taking away
from sensation this
removal of
emptiness

CM

ACKNOWLEDGMENTS

A selection of these poems have previously been published in *Tears in the Fence*. Endpaper images by Chris McCabe have previously featured in *M58* (www.m58.co.uk)

Quote from 'Night Thoughts' by David Gascoyne is taken from *Selected Poems* : Enitharmon Press, 1994.